Editor
Eric Migliaccio

Managing Editor
Ina Massler Levin, M.A.

Editor-in-Chief
Sharon Coan, M.S. Ed.

Illustrator
Kevin Barnes

Cover Artist
Brenda DiAntonis

Art Coordinator
Kevin Barnes

Art Director
CJae Froshay

Imaging
Craig Gunnell

Product Manager
Phil Garcia

Publisher
Mary D. Smith, M.S. Ed.

Beginning Writing

Grades K-2

My Autobiography

Hi! My name is David.

I was born in Apple Valley.

When I was a baby, I used to play with an orange teddy bear I named "Ba-Ba". was my favorite bear.

- Daily Writing
- The Writing Process
- Writing Genres
- Language Conventions

Includes Writing Samples!

Author

Sarah Kartchner Clark, M.A.

Teacher Created Resources

Teacher Created Resources, Inc.
6421 Industry Way
Westminster, CA 92683
www.teachercreated.com
ISBN 13: 978-0-7439-3223-3
ISBN 10: 0-7439-3223-4
©2004 Teacher Created Resources, Inc.
Reprinted, 2006
Made in U.S.A.

Table of Contents

Journal Writing—The Word Wall—Word Wall Activities—High Frequency Word Lists—
Writing Learning Centers—Daily Oral Language

Class Books—Class Newsletters—Beginning, Middle, and End—Get It Together!—
Autobiographical Writing—All About Me

Brainstorming Web—Venn Diagram—Check It Out!—First, Next, Then, Finally…

Narrative Writing Web—See the Picture—Personal Narrative Sample

Create a Character—Story Map—Story Sample

Book Report Form A—Book Report Form B—Book Report Sample

Model Letter—Letter Format—Letter Sample

Sentence Frames—Expository Idea Graph for Beginning Writers—Expository Sample

Language Use and Conventions—What Is a Sentence?—Tell Me Something—Put It All
Together!—What Is a Question?—Descriptive Language—Capitalization—Do It in Five!

Introduction

You are about to embark on a unit of study entitled *Beginning Writing*. This unit is geared for students in kindergarten, first, and second grade, or students at similar levels. Writing at this age is very new. Beginning writing can consist of squiggles on a page or writing a name for the first time. Children may not be able to read what they have written but they are learning to express themselves through the written word.

The beginning "texts" of students include material that is spoken, drawn, and acted out, along with attempts to print letters and words. The imaginations of children are well ahead of their writing skills. With this in mind, it is important to teach children how to write while allowing their creativity and personal expression to remain in tact.

The Writing Standards

Beginning Writing gives the teacher tools to help teach young children how to write. It is important that young writers be given instruction in how to write. Young writers also need exposure to different types of writing. The writing standards on page 8 will provide the framework for lessons and activities taught in this unit. These standards can also be used to document progress and growth.

Progress and Assessment

Portfolios are an excellent way of keeping track of student progress and student work. Teachers can record the progress of each student in the writing standards by using the "Student Writing Checklist" on page 9. Create a portfolio for each student. A writing portfolio can be easily made by stapling the "Student Writing Checklist" inside a manila folder and placing samples of writing texts inside for each student. Assemble portfolios before you begin the unit of study.

Keep the portfolios accessible for both the teacher and the students alike. Do not store them in the students' desks. They can easily get lost that way. Acknowledge progress and praise student work on a regular basis. Portfolios are essential to document the growth and achievement in the writing process.

Assessment is critical in this unit. Assessment needs to take place at various stages of writing. Use "Rubrics for Emergent Writers" (pages 22–24) to determine how well your students are learning and mastering the standards and objectives. The rubrics are designed to help show the next step for each student. "Stages, Levels, and Rubrics of Emergent Writers" (page 10) can also be used. The writing samples that follow are included to help teachers determine the stage and level of each student.

Preparation and Set Up

It is important for you to make preparations ahead of time for this unit. Look on page 4, "Setting Up a Writing Classroom," for classroom ideas for bulletin boards and other activities. Select the bulletin boards and activities that you would like to incorporate and prepare the materials needed for each of them.

Setting Up a Writing Classroom

As you set up your classroom, there are many things you can do to facilitate writing and writing activities in your classroom. Use the suggestions below to enrich the writing environment of your classroom.

✎ Daily Writing Activities

There are writing experiences that students should be exposed to every day. Daily exposure to these activities helps build a strong writing foundation and provides experience with writing. Select the daily writing activities from pages 25–35 to use in your classroom. These activities can be completed individually, with a partner or small group, or as a class.

✎ Journals

Writing in a journal is an easy way to get students to write every day. Writing in a journal allows students to write about their most familiar subject—themselves! Journals are easy and inexpensive to make. You can create a journal by stapling pages inside two pieces of construction paper or buying a small notebook for each student. Please keep in mind the stage of your students. The younger students need more basic pages. Early writers may not need lines at all on the page. As the year progresses, lines can be introduced. For more experienced writers, begin with lined paper, but keep in mind that students need more space between lines than are given in college-ruled notebooks. If you cannot find paper with appropriate space between lines, use a ruler to make your own lines and make copies of this page for the journals. See pages 25 and 26 for more information on journal writing.

✎ Word Walls

Designate an area of your wall space to be a "word wall." Word walls at this stage are a vital tool students can use in their writing. A word wall can help students get over the speed bumps of how to spell and write specific words. Word walls can be hung around the room on large sheets of laminated construction paper. (See pages 27–30 for word wall activities and for a list of high frequency words.) You can also set up another word wall to hold theme-specific words to help increase students' vocabulary on subjects you are studying in class.

✎ Writing Collection

Bring in a variety of writing samples for students to see. This collection should be placed in a prominent place. This writing collection should be posted on a bulletin board or collected in a tub or box. This writing collection could include letters, newspaper articles, postcards, notes, business letters, recipes, printed emails, business reports, calendars, brochures, menus, receipts, and any other type of writing used in our society. Encourage students to bring in samples (with permission) from home to add to the writing collection. Set aside a time for students to peruse the writing collection. Discuss different types of writing and how they are used with the students.

Setting Up a Writing Classroom *(cont.)*

✏ Bulletin Boards

It is important to have a place in your class to post student writing. This is a form of publishing for students. It also helps students share what they have written and learn about the audience to whom they are writing. Below are a few suggestions of bulletin boards that can be used in your classroom. Each bulletin board begins with colored paper and a colored border as a background.

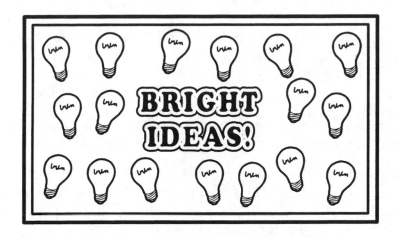

✏ Published Works!

The purpose of this bulletin board is to spotlight pieces of work that students have taken through the writing process. The writing process includes brainstorming, drafting, rewriting, editing, and finally publishing. Few writing assignments at this level actually go through this entire process. Posting the finished works helps to celebrate the writing and effort involved. These published pieces could also have an "About the Author" card with brief information listed, as well as a photograph of the author.

✏ Bright Ideas!

This bulletin board celebrates brainstorming and the thinking that goes into writing. Not all ideas for a story are written and not all information discussed gets placed in a report. Attach a light bulb to each bright idea and post it on the board for future use. Doing this can also validate the work and thought students put into the idea.

✏ The "Write" Stuff

Use this bulletin board to display all types of writing that you see your students doing. Post class works, as well as independent authors. When is the last time the teacher posted writing of his or her own? Don't forget to include that on this bulletin board as well.

✏ Our Writing Collection

Read the directions for the writing collection on page 4. This bulletin board can be used to display samples of writing found in the everyday environment. This bulletin board demonstrates all the different ways that writing is used. There are a variety of purposes, audiences, styles, and formats. Encourage students to bring samples from home to add to the writing collection.

Expectations for Emergent Writers

We know that young writers are limited in their writing because the physical act of forming letters and the concentration required to sound out and spell words can tire them out. What appears on the page of an emergent writer only hints at the rich composition early writers can do mentally. What can be expected of an early writer? There is a lot to be expected! Listed below are some expectations to consider.

1. **Write daily.**

   Writing should be formal as well as informal. Daily writing in a journal gives students practice writing in an unstructured environment. Some writing throughout the day should consist of formalized instruction. For example, you may spend time having students write complete sentences, use capitalization, or write a story. The skill may be specific or broad. These lessons build upon one another and will be reflected in student writing.

2. **Generate content and topics for writing.**

   Sometimes students will be given assigned content and topics for their writing in order to facilitate your writing curriculum. However, there should be opportunities throughout the day when students are allowed to generate their own content and topics. Following this practice teaches that writing is a way that we can communicate with others for a variety of reasons. We don't just write to fulfill school assignments. We write to express feelings and thoughts, to state opinions, to entertain, to inform, and to learn.

3. **Write without resistance when given the time, place, and materials.**

   Students should be allowed to write without too many restraints. As a teacher, your responsibility is to encourage writing in a non-threatening environment.

4. **Use whatever means are at hand to communicate and make meaning: drawings, scribbles, letter strings, letter approximations and other graphic representations, as well as gestures, intonations, and role-played voices.**

   Be aware that students begin verbally "writing" texts long before they actually begin writing. Writing comes in a variety of forms and stages. Encourage students to express themselves using several methods and means. Demonstrate how to express voice using oral and written language.

5. **Make an effort to reread their own writing and listen to that of others. Show attentiveness to meaning by, for example, asking for more information or laughing.**

   You will find with early writers that they are not always able to read what they have written. Encouraging students to read their own writing strengthens their skills and understanding of the written word. Listening to and reading the writing of others also widens the comprehension and the exposure that students receive. Given experience, students will seek out the written word and want to find the meaning therein.

Interactive Writing Settings

There are four main types of writing settings that take place in an elementary classroom. Each setting plays a specific role in strengthening the writing skills of students. Provide a variety of settings in your writing instruction.

✏ Modeled Writing

When the teacher models writing in front of her class, thinking aloud as he/she writes, this is called modeled writing. The teacher may be writing assignment directions, a note to the class, or a story. Modeling general writing as well as specific writing is key. When given a writing assignment, go through the complete process that students should follow in a modeled writing setting. The teacher says aloud what he or she is thinking as he or she is writing and explaining the process. This provides students with a clear understanding of the writing expectations, as well as an example of how to go about completing the writing assignments.

✏ Shared Writing

Shared writing is when students are encouraged to share ideas while the teacher does the writing. Often this type of writing lesson relates to a unit of study or book with which the entire class is familiar. This way, all students have similar background and knowledge on the subject. Shared Writing projects can include a class report, a class story, a class poem, and more. As the class works together to write the text, the teacher serves as the writer or scribe. Again, the class has a model of correct spelling, punctuation, grammar, and content, while using the thoughts and ideas of the students. The teacher should ask questions like, "What can I write about in the next sentence?" "Tell me a little bit more about what you mean?" "What should I put at the end of this sentence?" "What should we always begin a new sentence with?"

✏ Guided Writing

During a guided-writing lesson, the teacher works with small groups of students who have similar strengths and provides instruction through mini-lessons. The teacher can use modeling again with these small groups. The teacher is able to focus on the key areas and levels of these students. The teacher can encourage and challenge the students in areas specific to students' needs.

✏ Independent Writing

Students can write independently when they need very little support or when they are writing for the experience. Be sure that students who can work independently are given plenty of opportunity to do so. All students will do independent writing throughout their writing instruction, but it is important to make sure that early and emergent writers are not expected to write independently too soon without correct instruction and guidance on writing assignments. Daily activities such as journal writing, daily oral language, and brainstorming can be done independently, but there are assignments that should be given a lot of modeling and instruction before students are expected to write independently. Do not underestimate the importance of guided, modeled, and shared writing instruction.

Writing Standards and Skills
Grades K–2

It is important to know where students are and where they are going in their writing progression. These standards will give you a framework on which to plan lessons and assess student work. Some students will be able to master all of these standards, while other students will begin to incorporate these standards in their writing. Be sensitive to the stages and levels of emergent writers. (See page 10 for more information.) These standards will be taught and discussed in this unit, and they help to form the student checklist on page 9.

Standard 1: Uses general skills and strategies of the writing process

A. Uses prewriting strategies to plan written work.

B. Uses strategies to draft and revise written work.

C. Uses strategies to edit and publish written work.

D. Evaluates own and others' writings.

E. Uses strategies to organize written work. (Beginning, middle, end, sequencing)

F. Uses writing and other methods (drawing pictures, phonetic spelling, dictating, making lists) to describe people, places, and things.

G. Writes in a variety of forms of genres (e.g., picture books, letters, simple reports, personal experience narratives, stories, and more).

Standard 2: Uses the stylistic and rhetorical aspect of writing

A. Uses general and frequently used words to convey basic ideas.

Standard 3: Uses grammatical and mechanical conventions in written compositions

A. Forms letters in print and spaces words and sentences.

B. Uses complete sentences in written work.

C. Uses declarative and interrogative sentences.

D. Uses nouns in written work.

E. Uses verbs in written work.

F. Uses adjectives in written work.

G. Uses conventions of spelling (spells phonetically, uses consonant sounds, uses letter-sound relationships, spells basic short vowel words, and uses high-frequency words).

H. Uses conventions of capitalization in written work (first and last names, first word in a sentence).

I. Uses conventions of punctuation in written work (uses period, question mark, and commas in series of words).

Standard 4: Gathers and uses information for research purposes

A. Generates questions about topics of personal interest.

B. Uses books and resources to gather information (e.g., uses table of contents, examines pictures and charts).

Student Writing Checklist

Use this checklist to keep track of student progress. Use the columns to record dates or writing assignments and check whether standards and skills are being met.

Student Name: _____

1. Uses prewriting strategies to plan written work.						
2. Uses strategies to draft and revise written work.						
3. Uses strategies to edit and publish written work.						
4. Evaluates own and others' writings.						
5. Uses strategies to organize written work.						
6. Uses writing and other methods to describe people, places, objects, or experiences.						
7. Writes in a variety of forms or genres.						
8. Uses general and frequently used words to convey basic ideas.						
9. Forms letters in print and spaces words and sentences.						
10. Uses complete sentences in written work.						
11. Uses declarative and interrogative sentences.						
12. Uses nouns in written work.						
13. Uses verbs in written work.						
14. Uses adjectives in written work.						
15. Uses conventions of spelling.						
16. Uses conventions of capitalization in written work.						
17. Uses conventions of punctuation in written work.						
18. Generates questions about topics of personal interest.						
19. Uses books and resources to gather information.						

Stages, Levels, and Rubrics for Emergent Writers

✏ Stages

Each student is at a different level and stage with his or her writing. Knowing the stages of progress in emergent and early writers helps us comprehend the understanding of the student. Listed below are the stages of emergent and early writers:

Stage 1: I can think about something.

Stage 2: I can talk about what I think.

Stage 3: I can write about what I say.

Stage 4: I can read what I write.

Stage 5: Other people can read what I write, too.

Stage 6: I can affect the way other people think about things.

✏ Levels

Levels are more specific as to the ability of the student. Each student generally progresses through these levels. Some students pass through these levels quickly, while others progress more slowly. Outlined below is a brief description of each level:

Level 1: scribbles when drawing

Level 2: draws with some meaning

Level 3: scribbles when writing

Level 4: writes some letters

Level 5: writes or labels using words

Level 6: writes phrases

Level 7: writes a sentence phonetically

Level 8: writes a patterned sentence phonetically

Level 9: writes related sentences using phonetic/transitional spelling

Level 10: writes several sentences about one subject

Level 11: writes paragraphs

Pages 11–21 provide writing samples of each level listed above. You may want to use these samples to determine the levels at which your students are performing.

✏ Rubrics

When evaluating the writing of early and emergent writers, what should be considered? What does early and emergent writing look like? Included in the following pages are rubrics that you can use as a teacher to evaluate the writing of early and emergent writers. These rubrics look at the content and the conventions in each piece of writing. These forms can be adapted to meet the needs of each writing assignment. You will notice the rubrics have been separated into three phases. Kindergarten students typically demonstrate abilities listed in phase 1, while first-grade students use phase 2, and second-grade students would fit the criteria in phase 3. By using these rubrics, you will be able to see the progress of the students as they pass through stages and levels.

Student Writing Sample 1

Level 1

This student scribbles when drawing. There are no words, but the student is able to draw pictures.

Student Writing Sample 2

Level 2

The student draws with some meaning. The student draws pictures that are relevant to the topic and recognizes that pictures convey meaning.

(fish)

Student Writing Sample 3

Level 3

The student scribbles when writing. The student understands that print conveys meaning. The student writes top to bottom.

(scribble writing)

Student Writing Sample 4

Level 4

The student writes some letters. The student uses pictures and print to convey meaning. The student recognizes that print conveys meaning.

(Matt with his mom)

Student Writing Sample 5

Level 5

The student writes or labels using words. The student is able to write common words based on letter/sound relationships. The student is using all lowercase letters.

(cat, hen, tree)

Student Writing Sample 6

Level 6

The student writes phrases. The student writes common words based on letter/sound relationships. The student uses lowercase letters. The student uses pictures and print to convey meaning.

(one bird)

Student Writing Sample 7

Level 7

The student writes a complete thought. The student uses pictures and print to convey meaning. The student spells phonetically. The student uses one, two, or three letters to represent whole words.

(I walk a dog.)

Student Writing Sample 8

Level 8

The student writes a complete sentence. The student spells high frequency words correctly and uses knowledge of some word patterns to spell words correctly. The student uses developmental spelling with unfamiliar words. The student experiments with punctuation and capitalization. The student uses appropriate spacing between words.

(I like cats because I have two.)

Student Writing Sample 9

Level 9

The student spells high frequency words correctly. The student uses knowledge of some word patterns. The student writes related sentences using phonetic and transitional spelling. The student uses appropriate spacing between words. The student uses capital letters at the beginning of the sentence and at the beginning of names. The student uses ending marks correctly.

My nam is Bie.
I like it. I like
my beD.
Jessica

(My room is big. I like it. I like my bed)

Student Writing Sample 10

Level 10

The student writes several sentences about one subject. The student spells high frequency words correctly. The student uses knowledge of some word patterns to spell correctly. The student uses phonetic spelling with unfamiliar words. The student uses appropriate spacing. The student uses capital letters at the beginning of sentences and proper nouns. The student uses ending marks correctly.

We wnt to the zho and I went wth mi cuzn. We zaw the Trzan Muve. We at POPCORN. Yumme! Allizon

(We went to the show, and I went with my cousin.
We saw the Tarzan movie. We ate popcorn. Yummy!)

Student Writing Sample 11

Level 11

The student writes paragraphs on a specific topic. The student expresses ideas clearly. The student spells most common words correctly. The student uses strategies to help spell difficult words correctly. The student generally uses correct grammar and punctuation. The student experiments with transition. The student has begun to consider the audience to the writing. The student writes with features of focus, logical flow, and support or elaboration extended by details, examples, or descriptions. A teacher has written comments in the right margin.

> On Saturday I jumped on my trapline. I was still in my p.j.s. I was in a good mood. For breakfast I had cereal and yogert. Then me and Anne played pinorrs. She went to read I played all by myself the Anne went to basket ball. I went to a friends house. I had lunch there. At home I played horses. Then I jumped again.
>
> *Are you playing too?*
>
> On Sunday I jumped again. Then I got ready for a lunchen. I had a good lunch. Then I went to church. Afte I laughed for a good 10 minites. It drove Anne crazy! I had dinner after and cherry cobbuler! We had famliy night then I went to bed.
>
> *You are a silly willy*
>
> *mmm!*

(On Saturday I jumped on my trampoline. I was still in my p.j.s. I was in a good mood. For breakfast I had cereal and yogurt. Then me and Anne played pioneers. She went to read. I played all by myself. Then Anne went to basketball. I went to a friend's house. I had lunch there. At home I played horses. Then I jumped again.

On Sunday I jumped again. Then I got ready for a luncheon. I had a good lunch. I went to church. After I laughed for a good ten minutes. It drove Anne crazy! I had dinner after and cherry cobbler! We had family night and then I went to bed.)

Rubrics for Emergent Writers
Phase 1

Name of Student: _____

Writing Genre: _____

Place an **X** next to the description that best fits the writing of the student at that point in time. This page can be copied and attached to student writing.

Content

❑ **Beginning**   The student draws pictures that are relevant to the topic. The student understands that print conveys meaning.

❑ **Basic**   The student uses pictures and print to convey meaning. The student adds labels.

❑ **Proficient**   The student writes a complete thought.

❑ **Expert**   The student stays on the topic and writes multiple sentences. The student begins to write sentences with purposeful order.

Conventions

❑ **Beginning**   The student writes with scribble writing and letter-like figures. The student uses mostly uppercase letters.

❑ **Basic**   The student copies names and words. The student uses one, two, or three letters to represent whole words. The student is beginning to use some letter/sound relationships to write unfamiliar words, especially for the beginning and ending sounds.

❑ **Proficient**   The student writes common words based on letter/sound relationships. The student may still confuse some letter sounds. The student uses both upper and lowercase letters in writing. Student writes left to right and top to bottom. The student uses appropriate spacing.

❑ **Expert**   The student spells high frequency words correctly and uses knowledge of some word patterns to spell words correctly. The student uses developmental spelling with unfamiliar words. The student is starting to use punctuation and capitalization. The student spaces words appropriately.

Rubrics for Emergent Writers *(cont.)*
Phase 2

Name of Student: _____

Writing Genre: _____

Place an **X** next to the description that best fits the writing of the student at that point in time. This page can be copied and attached to student writing.

Content

❏ **Beginning** The student uses pictures and print to convey meaning. The student uses labels.

❏ **Basic** The student writes a complete thought or sentence.

❏ **Proficient** The student can stay on a topic. The student includes multiple sentences. The writing has a beginning, middle, and end.

❏ **Expert** The student maintains focus. The student uses some examples of support such as details, examples, and descriptions. The student writes sentences in order.

Conventions

❏ **Beginning** The student copies words and names. The student represents whole words with one, two, or three letters. The student shows evidence of understanding some sound/letter relationships.

❏ **Basic** The student can write his or her name and favorite words. The student writes common words based on letter/sound relationships. The student confuses some letter sounds. The student combines upper and lowercase letters. The student can write left to right and top to bottom. The student usually uses appropriate spacing. The student uses some punctuation and capitalization.

❏ **Proficient** The student uses appropriate spacing. The student uses many capital letters at the beginning of sentences and proper nouns. The student punctuates correctly.

The student can spell some high frequency words correctly. The student spells some words correctly. The student uses developmental spelling with unfamiliar words.

❏ **Expert** The student spells many high frequency words correctly. The student uses knowledge of common spelling patterns/rules to spell new words. The student uses capital letters at the beginning of sentences and proper nouns. The student punctuates correctly.

Rubrics for Emergent Writers *(cont.)*
Phase 3

Name of Student: _____

Writing Genre: _____

Place an **X** next to the description that best fits the writing of the student at that point in time. This page can be copied and attached to student writing.

Content

❏ **Beginning** The student writes a complete thought or sentence.

❏ **Basic** The student stays on topic. The student's writing includes multiple sentences. The writing has a beginning, middle, and end.

❏ **Proficient** The student can maintain focus throughout the writing. The student uses some details, examples, and descriptions.

❏ **Expert** The student expresses ideas clearly. The student's writing contains features of focus; logical flow; and support, details, examples, or descriptions. The student begins using transitions. The student is aware of an audience when writing. The student is beginning to include voice in writing.

Conventions

❏ **Beginning** The student writes common words based on letter/sound relationships. The student writes own name and favorite words. The student confuses some letter sounds. The student uses both upper and lowercase letters. The student writes left to right and top to bottom. The student usually uses appropriate spacing. The student begins to use punctuation and capitalization.

❏ **Basic** The student spells some high frequency words correctly. The student shows understanding of word patterns to spell words. The student uses developmental and appropriate spelling with unfamiliar words. The student uses appropriate spacing. The student uses capital letters at the beginning of sentences and proper nouns. The student ends sentences with punctuation.

❏ **Proficient** The student spells common words based on letter/sound relationships. However, the student may still confuse some letter sounds. The student combines upper and lowercase letters in writing.

❏ **Expert** The student spells high frequency words correctly and uses knowledge of some word patterns to spell words correctly. The student uses correct punctuation and capitalization. The student spaces writing correctly.

Journal Writing

Allowing time for students to write unstructured every day is key to a successful writing curriculum. See the instructions on page 4 on how to assemble journals for your students to use. Store journals in an accessible place and in a place where they will not be easily lost or get in the way of other schoolwork. Set aside a designated time each day for students to write in journals.

Provide all the necessary materials such as writing utensils, crayons, erasers, etc. You may select the topics that students write about each day, or you can vary it by inviting students to select their own topic or choose one for the class. The more proficient writers your students become, the more advanced the journal topics should be. Below and on page 26 are some journal entry suggestions beginning with basic to higher-level topics.

1. Tell me about you. What are you like?
2. What do you like to eat for breakfast?
3. What is your favorite color?
4. Do you have a pet?
5. What do you like to eat for dinner?
6. What are some of your favorite things to do?
7. Who are your friends?
8. What kind of books do you like to read?
9. What do you want to do when you grow up?
10. What was your best day?
11. What was your worst day?
12. What would you do if you had $100?
13. What is your favorite candy?
14. The best kind of pizza is . . .
15. On the playground, I like to . . .
16. If we go to the zoo, we will see . . .
17. I am happy when . . .
18. I am sad when . . .
19. If I could fly, I would . . .
20. I would like to meet . . .
21. The best time of day is . . .
22. If I were President, I would . . .
23. I'd like to invent . . .
24. Winter vacation was . . . because . . .
25. Summer vacation was . . . because . . .
26. I am . . .
27. I see . . .
28. I went . . .
29. I have . . .
30. It is . . .
31. I like to . . . because . . .
32. I can hardly wait to . . . because . . .

Journal Writing *(cont.)*

33. My favorite song to sing is . . . because . . .
34. My heart beats faster when I . . .
35. You can tell someone is kind when . . .
36. I know I am right/left handed because . . .
37. When I get my feelings hurt, I usually . . .
38. A place I would like to visit is . . .
39. My favorite number and letter are . . . because . . .
40. The biggest mess I ever made was . . .
41. Once I found a . . .
42. My friends help me . . .
43. A healthy snack is . . .
44. Something I have learned is . . .

45. My family helps me . . .
46. When I was younger, I didn't know how to . . .
47. To be safe, I . . .
48. If I were an animal, I would . . .
49. For my birthday, I want to . . .
50. I don't like to . . .
51. When I was a baby, I could . . .
52. If I were a clown, I would . . .
53. When my relatives come . . .
54. Before I go to school. . .
55. I am curious about . . . because . . .
56. Homework is . . . because . . .

✏ What Should I Do with the Journals?

There are many things that can be done with the journals. For many people, journals are considered private. At this age, most of the written work that children write is meant to be shared. Children at this age want to share parts of their life. They are not ashamed of who they are or what they have done. Allow time for students to share what they have written with others. It is good for students to listen to other students' writing and it allows all students to learn that print conveys meaning to an audience.

Students may share what they have written with the teacher, another student, in a small group, or in front of the class. Do not force a child to read it if they are not comfortable sharing what they have written. Keep the sharing light and comfortable. Getting students to read what they have written is important, and it forces them to make sense of their writing. Do not share journal writing every day. There may not be time for this and it may get routine. Be sure to pick a day where students go back and read previous journal entries. It's always fun to see progress and remember previous experiences!

The Word Wall

The word wall can be used to reinforce spelling and writing in your classroom. Look for ways you can incorporate activities using the word wall.

✏ **Word Wall Goals**

1. Word walls should support the teaching of words and how words are used in writing.

2. Word walls should foster reading and writing.

3. The word wall should provide reference support for children during their reading and writing.

4. The word wall should promote independence on the part of young writers as they work with words in writing and reading.

5. Word walls should provide a visual to help children remember connections between letters and words.

6. Word walls should develop a growing core of words that become part of a writer's reading and writing vocabulary.

✏ **Guidelines for Using a Word Wall**

1. Add words gradually. Do not put too many up at a time. With younger students add one or two at a time. Older students can handle up to five words a week. (See pages 29–30 for high frequency words to put on the word wall.)

2. Make words very accessible by putting them where every student can see them. Be sure that the word wall is in a prominent place in the classroom and is easily accessible.

3. Write the words in big, black letters. Be sure the words are printed neatly. You can use background colors for color words.

4. Be selective about what words go on the word wall, limiting additions to those common words that children use a lot in writing. Keep word walls separate if you are also using a word wall for theme-related words.

5. Use the words on the word walls in a variety of activities. Practice those words by chanting, writing, reading, singing, and spelling them.

6. Do a variety of review activities. Be sure to provide enough practice so that words on the word wall become easy for students to identify, read, and spell automatically.

7. Encourage students to use the words on the word wall in all of their writing activities. Make sure that word wall words are spelled correctly in any writing students do.

Word Wall Activities

Many activities can be done with the word wall. Select the activities listed below that best meet the needs of your students.

✏ See It, Say It, Chant It, Sing It, and Clap It!

Find as many different ways as you can to read and spell the words on the word wall. Students need to become very familiar with each of these words so that they can use them in their writing. Try to vary the way these words are read.

✏ What's at the End?

Locate words with similar endings. Discuss common word endings with students.

✏ Make a Sentence

Assign each student a word. Students must come up with a sentence for the assigned word.

✏ Be a Mind Reader

One student selects a word and begins to give clues. Class members try to guess the word being described. Clues can include the beginning and ending letter, what the word rhymes with, how many letters are in the word, etc.

✏ What's at the Beginning?

Locate all the words that begin with the same letter. Write the words on cards. Shuffle them and then have students place the cards in ABC order.

✏ Guess the Covered Word

Write sentences on the board using the word wall words. See if students can figure out the covered word.

✏ Call the Word—Find it First!

Call one or more students up to the word wall at a time. Call out a word; see if students can find it quickly.

✏ Seek and Find

Locate pieces of writing in newspapers, brochures, letters, business cards, etc. that contain word wall words. Students can highlight these words using a highlighter marker.

✏ Artistic Words

Students write the words with beans, pasta, alphabet stamps, magnetic stickers, play dough, or paint.

✏ Word Wall Chains

Cut strips of paper. Students write a letter on each strip. Staple strips together to form words.

High Frequency Word Lists

Here is a list of high frequency words that can be used on your word wall and in student writing. The words are listed in alphabetical order and progressively increase in difficulty.

List 1

a	I	my
and	in	see
can	is	the
go	it	to
he	look	we
will	you	

List 2

about	his	said
all	into	she
around	know	show
ask	little	so
at	let	some
away	like	soon
big	make	stop
blue	may	take
but	me	that
call	new	then
come	no	they
did	not	this
do	now	to
down	of	two
eat	on	up
fast	one	us
for	out	want
from	play	went
good	put	what
green	ran	who
has	red	with
have	run	work
help	saw	yes
him	say	your

List 3

after	another	before
again	any	began
am	as	better
an	be	black

High Frequency Word Lists (cont.)

List 3 (cont.)

bring	never	should
by	next	tell
came	old	than
could	our	their
cut	read	them
does	still	there
don't	cold	these
find	didn't	think
first	far	those
found	five	three
four	gave	told
give	gone	took
going	hard	try
got	now	under
had	just	very
her	light	walk
hold	many	was
if	must	were
its	of	when
kind	off	where
last	or	which
long	other	white
made	over	why
more	own	would
much	right	

List 4

across	always	are
because	been	best
both	close	done
draw	enough	even
every	full	get
grow	heard	here
high	hot	I'm
keep	leave	left
mean	might	most
near	need	once
only	open	round
same	short	six
small	start	ten
thought	through	today
together	toward	turn
upon	use	warm
well	while	yet

Writing Learning Centers

Writing centers are a great way to reinforce skills you are teaching as a class. Writing centers also give students more practice writing in an informal and fun setting. Select the learning centers from this page or create your own that best meet the needs of your students. Be sure to vary the type of learning centers you use to meet the different learning styles of your students.

✏ A Letter a Day . . .

Place a collection of familiar books for students to read. Once finished, students will write a letter to one of the characters in the story. Have paper and writing utensils available. What could they say in the letter? When finished, have students place their letters in an envelope and attach a sticker for a stamp. Students can place their letters in your classroom mailbox. (If time permits, you may respond to student letters.)

✏ Poetry Pizazz

Supply paper, crayons, and other materials needed for students to write a poem about a person in their family. Students may draw pictures in place of words if necessary. Students may use other poems as a guide, or they may create a new format.

✏ From the Kitchen

Make recipe cards and writing utensils available for students to write their own recipe for how to make cookies. What ingredients are needed? How much of each ingredient? How are they cooked? Once students have written the directions, they can draw pictures to help clarify the directions in their recipes.

✏ Word Rings

Provide rings and index cards for each student. Punch a hole in each index card and create word rings. Students can write down high frequency words or words from their writing. After the words have been written and added to the ring, students can practice reading the words. Students can keep the word rings handy for when they are writing.

✏ Letter Books

Select a letter of focus from your instruction for students to work on. Have little books available for students to paste the letters they find to create a letter book. Then ask students to look through magazines and locate pictures that begin with this letter. Students should paste the letters they find in their books. Students can also paste words that begin with this letter in their books.

✏ Play Dough Duty

Have play dough available for students to spell words from a poem or short story. Be sure to have poems or stories posted on poster paper for student reference. It will be difficult for students to work with play dough and turn the pages of a book. Students may also practice making the words from the classroom Word Wall.

Writing Learning Centers *(cont.)*

✐ A Self Portrait

Have mirrors available at this center for students to look at. How would students define themselves? Have students draw a picture of themselves. Have students use describing words to describe themselves. Students do not need to write sentences, but describing words.

✐ Character Analysis

Read a book aloud to the class before sending them to this center. Have students write a story about a character from the book you read. Have students draw a picture of the character at school, or in the store, or at the park, etc. What did the character do? What happened? Have pre-constructed blank little books available for students to illustrate the story. You can assist students, as necessary, with words and sentences. Be sure to have students determine a title and cover for their little book.

✐ Dicey Descriptions

Supply paper, crayons, and other materials needed for students to write a description about an object in the classroom. Students may draw pictures in place of words if necessary. If volunteer help is available, have students dictate their descriptions to the parent. Post a poster with an example of a description at this center. At a later time, read the student descriptions aloud to the class and see if the class can name the object from its description.

✐ Recording the Voice

This center will need volunteer help. Have a tape player available to students and have them read or tell a story into the tape player. The volunteer can assist the students in pressing record and stop. Encourage students to use expression as they speak. Allow time later in class to play the tape so that students can hear themselves.

✐ Labels, Labels, Labels

Have index cards, masking tape, and colored markers available at this center. Students are to make labels for objects in the classroom. Students may use inventive spelling or phonetic spelling in their labels. A volunteer could be used to assist students in fastening tape and posting the labels.

✐ Look and Locate

Have magazines, glue, pieces of construction paper, and scissors available at this center. Provide plenty of magazines for students to peruse and cut. Students should look for nouns. Once nouns have been found, have students cut them out and glue them to a piece of construction paper. At a future center, you can give students their noun pages and select one of the nouns on which to write a story.

Writing Learning Centers *(cont.)*

✏ You Be the Teacher!

Ask students to write about an experience they have had learning to do something all by themselves. Perhaps this was the first time they rode their bike without training wheels or tied their shoes. Provide paper and writing materials at this center. Have students write as many words as they can about the experience. Then have students illustrate their experience to provide more details. Allow time for students to "teach" another student using their instructional page.

✏ One, Two, Buckle My Shoe

Have play dough available for students to spell number words and color words. Students can make the color words using the correct color of play dough. Once students have written number words, students can make items of the same number out of the play dough. Be sure to have number and color words available for student reference.

✏ A Family Portrait

Have paper and writing utensils available for students to make a book about their families. Students should draw a picture of each person in their families. Students can bind the pages together by punching three holes and then tying these with yarn.

✏ What Time Is It?

Make a clock available for students to look at and explore. Make small books with blank pages for students to write their own story about time. Have students draw hour-by-hour pictures of what they do. What do they do in the morning, noon, and night? This activity will assist with beginning, middle, and ending concepts. Have crayons available for students to illustrate their little books.

✏ Put It In Order!

Have sentence strips containing the lines from a familiar poem. At this center, have students work together to read the sentences and figure out the sequence of the poem. Have a book of this poem available for students to check their work or to use as needed.

✏ Down on the Farm

Display nonfiction books, magazine articles, and posters about farm animals. Have students browse these materials to learn more about farm animals. Arrange a time during the day to have students report to the class what they have learned about farm animals. The next day, have small books with blank pages prepared for students to "write a report" on what they have learned about farm animals.

✏ Reading = Writing

Set up an area in your room for independent reading. You can place beanbags, pillow, or chairs for more comfort. Keep a bookshelf of books available at all times for students to read and browse. Giving students time to read allows them to see capitalization, correct punctuation, and spelling, and they will begin to recognize words they can use in their writing.

Writing Learning Centers *(cont.)*

✏ Silly Sentences

Provide students with strips of paper and pencils. At this center, instruct students to write sentences. Explain to students that some of the sentences should be factual, while others will be silly and untrue. For example, a factual sentence might be, "Elephants are big animals." A silly sentence might read, "Elephants sleep in pajamas." Remind students to remember capitals and periods/question marks in the sentences. When finished, have students share their sentences with other students at this center. Which sentences are true? Which are false?

✏ Clay Critters

Provide clay at this learning center for students to mold and create his or her figure. The figure can be an animal, himself or herself, or any other object. When the sculpture has been completed, the student then writes five words describing the clay figure.

✏ Punctuate with Pasta

Provide paper and pencils at this center. Students should write a sentence. Using pasta shapes, the student will glue on punctuation where necessary. The students can make periods, question marks, or other punctuation marks, such as commas.

✏ A Day in the Life of…

Provide small booklets with blank pages at this center. On each page of the little book, have the students draw pictures of what they do in the morning, afternoon, and night. Instruct students to write sentences to accompany their pictures.

✏ Vocabulary Venue

On a piece of poster paper, write a word with an illustration in the middle. At this center, students will write down words that describe or are associated with the word written in the middle. For example, if the word in the middle would read "banana," students would add words to the poster like *tasty*, *yellow*, *squishy*, *peel*, *snack*, *pie*, *yummy*, *eat*, and *soft*.

✏ A Picture Is Worth 1,000 Words

Provide cutout pictures from magazines and other sources. When students come to this center, they will choose one of the pictures. Using the picture for inspiration, students will write a short story about what is in the picture. Be sure to allow time for students to share their stories. You may need to have a volunteer available to help some students with their writing.

✏ Dictionary Drill

Post a list of high-frequency words at this center. Place several children's dictionaries at the center for students to use. The students look up each word on the list. Students can work with a partner or independently. Have students read and determine the meaning of the word. Allow time for students to share their findings as a class or with you or another adult. Discuss the meaning of these words as a class. This will reinforce the use of these high-frequency words in student writing.

34

Daily Oral Language

An efficient way to address language conventions on a daily basis is to participate in daily oral language. Each day, as the students enter the classroom, have a sentence on the chalkboard or whiteboard that is not written correctly. Select one error a day. The error may include spelling, punctuation, capitalization, letter format, and more. As the students progress in their understanding of these things, you can begin to add more than one error to the sentence and you can add more than one sentence with errors.

As a class, orally read the sentence. Ask students to identify the errors in the sentence. Cross out the errors and write the corrections using different colored chalk or markers.

The daily oral language experience helps students to identify problems and learn how to correct writing. This daily skill reinforces the need for revision and editing of our writing. Teach children how to use resources to fix writing errors. Some of these resources might include the word wall, the teacher, a dictionary, past experience, etc. Here are some examples of sentences you can use.

Example: My school is red.   *Fixed:* My school is red.

1. I am tall _____

2. My catt is nice. _____

3. Where is mi teacher? _____

4. The box is beg. _____

5. How old are u? _____

6. The grapes are grean. _____

7. There is a bug The bug looks beeg _____

_____

8. My sister is fife and I am sevin and a half years old _____

_____

9. The horz makes a loud noise. He makes me laff. _____

_____

10. The snake slid across the flor. I is scared. _____

_____

11. I wnt to my gramas hose. She made cuukies. I love my grama _____

_____

Class Books

Class books are a fun way to encourage writing, and they can be made in a variety of ways. Here are a few suggestions:

- Each day provide a sentence which the student completes by adding several words. The student then illustrates the completed sentence. Staple the pages together to create a class book. Select a title that best fits the content of your book to go on the cover page.

- Provide a copy of the same illustration to each student in your class. The student colors the illustration and provides his or her own text to the illustration. Staple the pages together to create a class book. Select a title that best fits the content of your book to go on the cover page.

- On a piece of paper, provide talking bubbles as part of an illustration that can be used for writing on each child's page. What are the people or animals saying? Encourage the students to show humor. This humorous book will provide many giggles. Staple the pages together to create a class book. Select a title that best fits the content of your book to go on the cover page.

- Select a topic for the class book. Hold a discussion as a class to talk about ideas related to this topic. Assign each student a page to complete on this topic and to illustrate their ideas. Staple the pages together to create a class book. Select a title that best fits the content of your book to go on the cover page. For a more simplified version, a picture on a specific topic can be drawn by the student, and labeled by the student or teacher. Topics might include a letter, a food, a sport, an activity, family, and so forth.

- Alphabet books are easy to compile. Alphabet books have one letter per page. Each student is given a different letter. The subjects can be words that begin with the letter, nouns that begin with the letter, verbs that begin with the letter, types of animals, types of foods, and so forth. Staple the pages together to create a class book. Select a title that best fits the content of your book to go on the cover page.

- A script or story can be divided into parts, and each student can illustrate his or her story section or line of script. Be sure to read the class book aloud. Staple the pages together to create a class book. Select a title that best fits the content of your book to go on the cover page.

Class books can also be a collection of poems, stories, and texts written by students. If you do a class book at least once a week, by the end of the year, you should have one class book for each student to take home.

Class Newsletters

On a weekly basis, work with your students to create a class newsletter. Creating a newsletter is a great way to teach about audience and voice. The audience is the parents of the students. What would parents want to know about the classroom? What important and interesting facts should be shared? Work as a class to create a newsletter that involves each student. You can have each student write a sentence.

The next two pages are formats you can use for class newsletters.

Our Classroom News

In the news...

Today's Latest Information

Did You Know?

For Your Information

Class Newsletters *(cont.)*

What's Happening

Newsletter from ________________________'s Class

Here are some highlights from the week of ______________________ in our class!

Reporters: ____

____

Monday →

Tuesday →

Wednesday →

Thursday →

Friday →

Extra News and Notes: ____

____

____

Beginning, Middle, and End

Sequencing is an important skill for emergent writers to learn and use. It's not uncommon for early and emergent writers to neglect order in their writing. Sentences are written without any concern for sequencing or purposeful order. Sharing stories aloud, emphasizing the beginning, middle, and end is one exercise that can be helpful. Complete the following activity with students.

Directions

1. Cut along the dotted lines below. Place the pictures in order from beginning, middle, and end. See the sample.

2. Write a sentence telling what has happened in each of these pictures.

3. How do you know which picture comes first, second, and last? What if the ending was put first? Why does it matter if we write things in order?

4. Draw pictures in each square below and place them in order. Cut the squares out. Write a sentence explaining each picture.

Get It Together!

Look at the parts of the story below. All the parts are mixed up. Rearrange the story so that it is in order. Write the story correctly on the lines below.

Then, I looked under the table.

The Lost Cat

There was my cat sitting in the closet!

Finally I looked in the closet.

First, I looked under my bed.

This morning my cat got lost.

_____

_____

_____

_____

_____

_____

_____

_____

_____

Autobiographical Writing

Writing about one's self can build self-esteem and involve nonfiction writing. Emergent writers usually enjoy this type of writing because they are comfortable and familiar with the topic. They also enjoy talking about themselves and their viewpoint. Have students write a personal history of their lives . . . so far. Use the framework below to help students organize the information.

My Memories

Hi! My name is _____

I was born in _____

_____

A funny story about me is _____

_____

_____

When I was a baby, I used to play with _____

_____

_____

This year, I want to learn how to _____

_____

_____

All About Me

_____
Name

Draw a picture of yourself. Then fill in the blanks about you.

With my [mouth] I like to eat

_____ .

With my [hand] , I like to

_____ .

With my [eye] , I like to see

_____ .

With my [nose] , I like to smell

_____ .

With my [arm] , I like to

_____ .

With my [feet] , I like to

_____ .

I like to think [brain] about

_____ .

With my [ear] , I like to hear

_____ .

The Writing Process

The writing process helps the writer take a piece of writing from beginning or brainstorming to the end of the published piece. The writing process at the emergent writing level is done as a group though on occasion it is done individually. What makes up the writing process? The writing process includes brainstorming/prewriting, drafting, editing/revising, publishing, and reflection. Read the description of the writing process steps below. There are different points to consider at each step of the writing process. For emergent and early writers, not all pieces of writing will go through the complete writing process. As a teacher, be selective as to the writing assignments that will complete the writing process.

```
Brainstorming/Prewriting  ───────▶  Drafting  ────┐
                                                   │
                                                   ▼
Reflection  ◀───────  Publishing  ◀───────  Editing/Revising
```

☞ Brainstorming/Prewriting

This is the beginning phase where all writings begin. At this stage, writers are generating ideas, brainstorming topics, webbing ideas together, or just talking or thinking about ideas. For a specific piece of writing, the prewriting phase is important as it sets the foundation. Explain that students may get ideas for writing from personal experiences, stories, pictures, and a variety of sources. Encourage students to think about writing topics every day.

What does brainstorming and prewriting for early and emergent writers look like?

- discussions with teacher, partner, or class
- brainstorming individually, as a class, or with a partner
- using webbing or other graphics independently or as a group
- composing orally

☞ Drafting

At this stage of the process, students are beginning to get their ideas on paper. Generally, students need instruction on what should be written (i.e. is it a story? a narrative? a report?) For beginning writers, pictures and drawings may very well be part of the composition. Encourage students to write as much as they can on their own. Pieces of writing taken through the writing process should not be dictated or written by others. It should be the student's work throughout the process.

What does drafting for early and emergent writers look like?

- dictate writing ideas to adults or proficient writers
- copy information written by adults or proficient writers
- drafting done by students, who are writing words and ideas independently. Pictures and drawings may accompany text.

The Writing Process *(cont.)*

✏ Editing/Revising

At this phase, there are two parts. Editing looks at the mechanics of writing, while revision looks at the organization and the structure of the writing. Teach students how to look at both sides of the writing at this stage. This is the polishing part of the process. At this stage, students look back on what they have written and ask questions of their writing. Editing and revising forces the writer to look at their writing with a different point of view. Here are questions to consider when editing and revising:

- Read your own work backwards. Does each sentence make sense?
- Is there a word that needs to be added?
- Do you see or hear any errors in the sentence?

What does editing and revising for early and emergent writers look like?

- conference (peer/teacher)
- read and revise (student)

✏ Publishing

Publishing occurs when the other steps are completed and the student is ready to write his or her final copy. The final copy can be handwritten, typed, or word-processed. At this age, you may need to consider the abilities of your students. The goal is to present the information attractively so others can enjoy it.

What does publishing for early and emergent writers look like?

- create final copy (Student publishes a book that is typed and bound to look "professional.")
- share orally (Students read aloud to partner, group, or class.)
- publish "in-house" (Post on a bulletin board or in a class book.)

✏ Reflection

Reflection is a key phase in the writing process. It encourages the writer to look at his or her writing. Reflection helps the writer to look at his or her writing from a different point of view. Reflection allows the writer to see progress in his or her writing efforts. Reflection also allows the writer to look back at the brainstorming and the beginning of the writing project and check to see if the goals in this piece of writing were met.

What does reflection for early and emergent writers look like?

- student reads what has been written and asks questions like:
  - —"Is that what I wanted to say?"
  - —"Is there more that I want to tell?"
  - —"Which is my favorite part in this writing?"
  - —"Did I write it the way I planned to write this piece?"
- students are given opportunities to read/share their writing with others.

Brainstorming Web

Use this brainstorming web to record your thoughts and ideas.

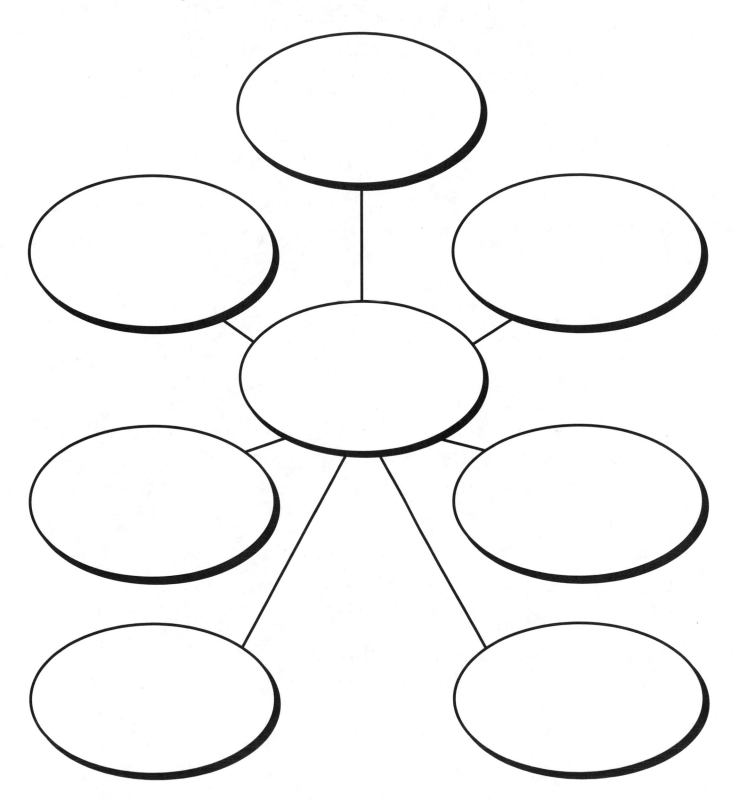

Venn Diagram

A Venn diagram can help compare two different items or ideas. Use a Venn diagram to help generate descriptive words in comparison. For younger students, begin using the Venn diagram as a class, then in small groups, and finally independently.

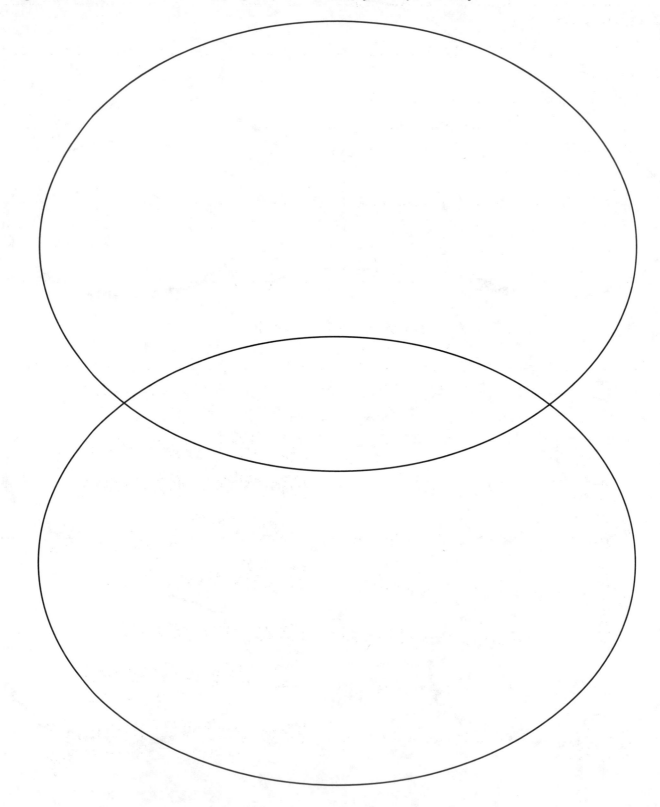

Check It Out!

This page can be used to assist students in the editing and revising portion of the writing process.

	Yes	No
Capitalization Did you capitalize the first word of each sentence?		
Punctuation Did you put a period (.) or question mark (?) at the end of each sentence?		
Handwriting Did you write neatly? Can it be neater?		
Spelling Did you check your spelling? How can you figure out how to spell these words?		

Proofreading Marks

Use these proofreading marks to show where changes need to be made in student writing. Review and practice these marks with students so they become familiar with their meaning.

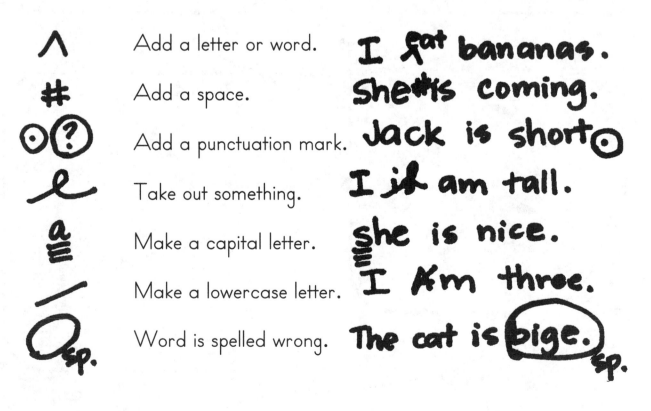

First, Next, Then, Finally...

Use this graphic organizer to help your students write things sequentially. This can be used with fiction as well as nonfiction writing.

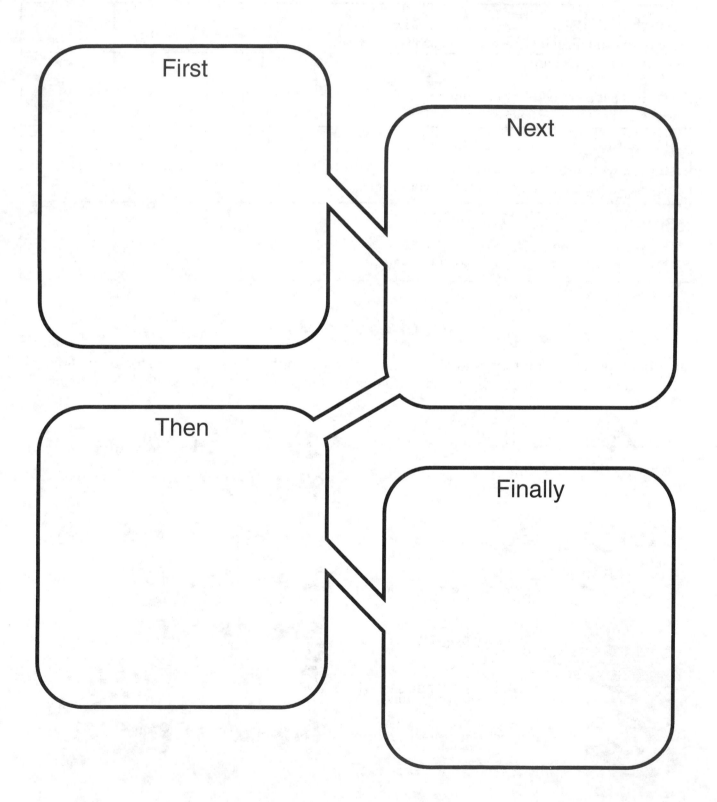

First

Next

Then

Finally

Types of Writing for Emergent Writers

Exposing students to the different types of writing can help expand their writing skills and abilities. It is important to select writing activities that are relevant for beginning writers. One of the goals of these writing assignments is to teach beginning writers that writing communicates meaning. There are a variety of writing activities that encourage the expression of meaning. Beginning writers should also write for a variety of purposes and write to a variety of audiences.

The writing assignments selected in this unit have these goals in mind. These writing assignments should be modified to meet the needs of your students and can be completed individually, with a partner, or as a group. Here are the different types of writing genres and types of writing in each genre. This unit will provide lessons and formats for teaching how to write a narrative, story, book report, personal letter, and an expository piece. Remember that all of these writing assignments will be modified to meet the individual needs of your students.

General Writing Expectations

- Write left to right, write name, write letters from A–Z and numerals from 0–9, label drawings, and write sentences

Personal Narrative

- Write a story from personal experience
- Describe events from direct experience or observation

Writing a Story

- Write sensory words to describe something
- Write a story about a familiar character or person
- Make up new characters and write a story about them

Responding to Literature

- Retell stories heard
- Write a book report
- Write a new ending to a story

Writing a Letter

- Write a thank-you note
- Compose signs and labels for the classroom
- Write a letter to a friend or family member

Expository Writing

- Dictate questions for field trips or visitors
- Collect and record data about the weather
- Create a set of rules for an outdoor game
- Make a list of supplies needed for a class party
- Write a procedure for lunch, clean-up, snack, etc.

Writing a Personal Narrative

Use this lesson to introduce how to write a personal narrative. The objective of this lesson is to write a personal narrative as a class.

Materials

- copies of "Narrative Writing Web" (page 51)
- copies of "See the Picture" (page 52)
- chart paper
- marking pen

Preparation

Create an experience for your students such as going on a tour of the school, watching an interesting play or puppet show, going on a scavenger hunt for specified items, or watching a group of ants.

Directions

1. In order for students to write a personal narrative, the students are asked to tell what happened from personal experience or describe a series of events in chronological order. The author tells about a personal experience, describing the event and his or her reactions or feelings about what happened.

2. Review the things to remember about personal narrative writing:

   - first-person point of view (I, we)
   - chronological organization (events unfold as they happened)
   - significance of events is revealed
   - reader shares thoughts and feelings
   - the setting (time and place are clear)
   - people involved are described and developed

3. Once you have finished the "experience" as a class, you are ready to write the narrative. Ask students to close their eyes and picture the experience. What do they remember? What did they see? What did they hear? What did they feel? What did they smell? Using the senses can really help students capture the experience in writing.

4. Record student responses on the chart paper with the colored marker. Once all of the ideas have been recorded, you are ready to write the narrative. Use the notes to help write the narrative. Remember to use the first person point of view. Think aloud as you write. Encourage students to suggest a sentence to add to the narrative.

5. Once you have finished the narrative, read the narrative aloud to the students. Ask students if there is any more information or clarification about the experience that needs to be added. Look back over the narrative for capitalization and punctuation. Ask students to draw illustrations to accompany this narrative.

Narrative Writing Web

Use this graphic to organize your information about an experience. The inner rectangle contains the name of the experience. The ovals contain the events. The outer rectangles record the description and feelings regarding each event.

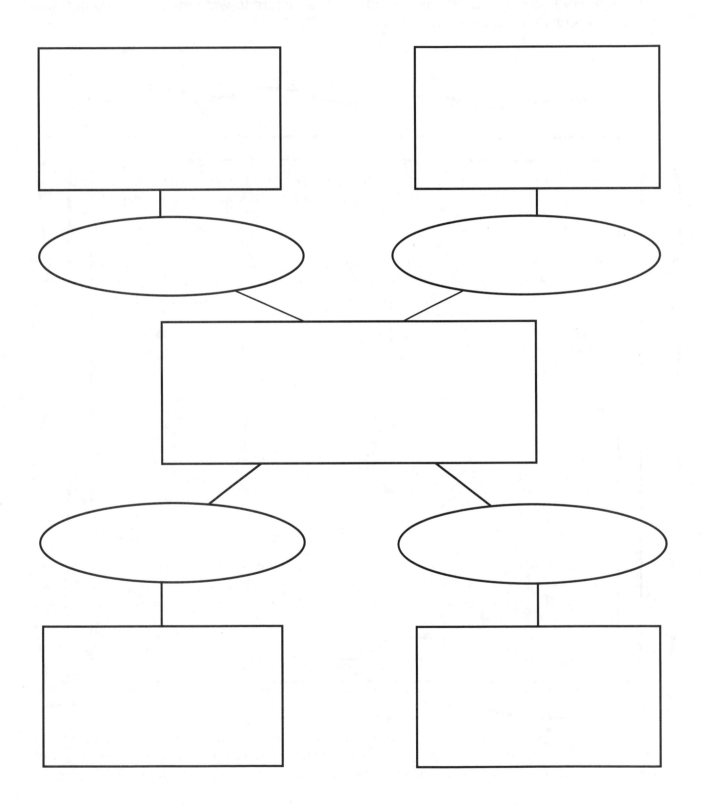

See the Picture

For early and emergent writers, it is easier to write about what happened after they have drawn a picture. Use the frame to help focus the students' ideas. As students draw their pictures, encourage them to draw as many details as possible. Ask questions to encourage students to be very specific. Students should use this picture to write their personal narrative. Encourage students to refer to the picture as they write.

Personal Narrative Sample

A second grade student at the midpoint of the school year wrote this sample of a personal narrative. The student uses complete sentences. Periods are used inconsistently and the spacing is uneven. Some of the letters are uppercase when they should be lowercase. The text is readable by adults who are familiar with phonetic spelling. Additionally, a number of high-frequency words are spelled correctly.

Saturday morning I went To a Soccer game We won. me an Skyler Brakston and Brooke We eche got a prise it was so fun I got more points than Skyler he got ten pirts I got twentyoa pints. On Sunday I went out Side to Shoot Basket Balls in the hoop I allmost shot a hoop it mist. it Started to get boring my mom i called Let goto Golden corral to eat brecfast there was So much to eat I took the hash brows, SoseJ, eges, water melon, doute, Iicrem, pancaK, waffuls, Iicrem cone, pizza.

(Saturday morning I went to a soccer game. We won. Me and Skyler, Braxston, and Brooke, we each got a prize. It was so fun. I got more points than Skyler. He got ten points. I got twenty–one points.

On Saturday I went outside to shoot basketballs into the hoop. It missed. It started to get boring. My mom called, "Let's go to Golden Corral to eat breakfast." There was so much to eat. I took the hash browns, sausage, eggs, watermelon, donuts, ice cream, pancakes, waffles, ice cream cones, and pizza.)

Writing a Story

Use this lesson to introduce how to write a story. The objective of this lesson is to write a story as a class.

Materials

- short story to use as a model story
- chart paper
- colored marker
- copies of "Create a Character" (page 55)
- copies of "Story Map" (page 56)

Directions

1. Read the book you have selected to the class. Discuss the elements of a story with students. What does a story have?

   - setting
   - problem
   - characters
   - solution

2. Read the title of the book with the students, pointing out the location of the capital and lowercase letters. Read the names of the author and illustrator, pointing out that the author and the illustrator are usually two different people.

3. Explain that a story has a beginning, middle, and an end. The beginning usually contains the setting and the introduction of the characters. The reader learns more about the characters and the problem in the middle of the story. The ending usually contains the solution to the problem.

4. Work together as a class to write a story. Record student ideas on the chart paper using the marking pen. First, discuss the characters. Which characters should be in the story? To get a better idea of the characters, have students illustrate a picture of a character using the character face on page 55. As a class, select the characters to be in the story. Remember to keep the number of characters limited.

5. Now, move to the setting. Brainstorm locations where the setting takes place. Locations might be home, school, playground, movie theater, or the store. Brainstorm problems for the story. Problems might be someone getting lost, being scared, getting hurt, or losing something. Now you are ready to write. Write each sentence as a class. Call on one student at a time to add to the story. Once the story has been written, read it to the class. Discuss changes needed. Instruct students to illustrate scenes from the story. Bind your story together when it is completed. Discuss a title as a class.

6. Explain to students that they are now ready to write a story of their own. Go through this same procedure to walk students through their own story. Use the story map on page 56 as a guide.

Create a Character

Story Map

Use this story map to help you plan your story. Follow the arrows to the next step.

Setting (*Where and when does the story take place?*)

Characters (*Who are the people/animals in the story?*)

Problem (*What is wrong in the story?*)

Action/Events (*What happens?*)

Solution (*How does the story end?*)

Story Sample

A first grade student at the midpoint of the school year wrote this sample of a story. The student uses complete sentences with proper capitalization and punctuation. This text is readable by adults who are familiar with phonetic spelling. Additionally, a number of high-frequency words are spelled correctly. The student introduces the character at the beginning of the story. The story contains a beginning, middle, and end, though the story is underdeveloped.

My name is Mousy mouse. Once I was sleeping in a grils perse and I came home with her, But she never saw me. But One day there was something stickey in there, So she took evething out except me. So she put her perse intehe Washing machine, and I got stuck in there. When she took evething out I snuck out, and I lived ih her bed, and I lived in here Sheets forever,

the End

(My name is Mousey Mouse. Once I was sleeping in a girl's purse and I came home with her. But she never saw me. But one day there was something sticky in there. So she took everything out except me. So she put her purse in the washing machine, and I got stuck in there. When she took everything out I snuck out and I lived in her bed. And I lived in her sheets forever. The End)

Responding to Literature

It is important for early and emergent writers to be exposed to writing. Exposure to writing models correct writing for the student and it encourages the student to listen to new ideas and viewpoints. Use the suggestions on this page to introduce how to respond to literature by writing a book report. When completed, select one of the book reports on pages 59–60 for your students to complete. Form A is basic while Form B is a little more advanced. Select the appropriate form for each of your students.

✎ Read Aloud

Read from a story each day to your students. Before, during, and after reading, discuss the story with the students. Expose your students to as many different types of literature as you possibly can. Get students talking, reading, and writing about literature!

✎ Give Me Five!

Trace around the hand of each student. The student needs to write five words describing a story he or she read. In the palm of the hand, have the student draw a picture about the story.

✎ Reports on File

Manila folders work great for students to draw a story map of what happened. Open up the folder and students can map out the story in sequence. What happened first? Have students draw arrows to show the direction he or she is heading. What happened next?

✎ Bag It!

Using a paper bag, have students design a face for a character from a story. Students will enjoy sharing information about the story when they pretend to be one of the characters. Students can use crayons, colored markers, and construction paper to decorate the bag. Unleash the creativity!

✎ Solve the Puzzle

Use a marker to divide a sheet of construction paper into puzzle-shaped pieces. Have students draw an event from the story in each section. Have students cut out the puzzle pieces and store them in a plastic bag. Have students exchange their puzzles with another student.

✎ Character Mobile

Create a character mobile using a plastic coat hanger. Students can draw pictures of characters from a story on construction paper. Cut the pictures out and hang them from the hanger with string.

✎ Take Five!

Videotape your students telling you about the book report. Students can dress up like reporters to make it official. Students will love to see themselves on camera reporting the details of their favorite story. Remind students to include all the elements of a story in their report.

Book Report Form A

Note to the teacher: This is a beginner form. Use Form B on page 60 for more advanced writers.

My name

_____

....

_____

Name of the book

_____

....

_____

Who wrote it (author)

_____

....

_____

A picture from my book

Book Report Form B

My name

_____
....
_____

Name of the book

_____
....
_____

Who wrote it (author)

_____
....
_____

Here are the faces of the main characters in the book.

( ) ( ) ( ) ( )

Here is a picture from the story.

I liked this book because . . .

_____
....
_____
_____
....

Book Report Sample

A second grade student at the midpoint of the school year wrote this sample book report. This is a more advanced book report. Book Report Forms A and B can be used with students beginning to write book reports. The student uses complete sentences with proper capitalization and punctuation. The student uses a title and discusses the characters and plot of the story. Many high-frequency words are spelled correctly.

[Handwritten sample:]

Summer Camp Caper

Carrtors
Ahsley and, Marykate, Tim, and there bunkmate
There trying to make Mary-kate go home.
But Who?

Suspects
Jodis, and Jackie because theiy want there
bunks back. Clark because he never got
any treats at home.

How to proof it?
Clark is allergick to nuts, did he steal
the nuts, and the treats? Read it and youll
find out!

I liked this book because its
a mistry, and I like to put cases
together!

Summer Camp Caper

Characters

Ashley, Mary Kate, Tim, and their bunkmates. They are trying to make Mary Kate go home. But who?

Suspects

Jody and Jackie because they want their bunks back. Clark because he never got any treats at home.

How to Prove It?

Clark is allergic to nuts. Did he steal the nuts and the treats? Read it and you'll find out!

I liked this book because it's a mystery and I like to put cases together!

Writing a Letter

Use this lesson to introduce how to write a letter. The objective of this lesson is to write a letter as a class.

Materials

- chart paper
- postage
- marking pen
- large envelope
- copies of "Letter Format" (page 64)
- overhead projector
- transparency of "Model Letter" (page 63)

Preparation

Prior to this lesson, make arrangements with a business, public library, grocery store, or other business to receive a letter from your class with the expectation that the business will respond with a letter.

Directions

1. For early and emergent writers, the letter written will be less formal. The format for the letter will follow the basic format on page 64 ("Letter Format"). Begin by explaining to your students that you will be writing a letter from your class to a business in town. Explain the business you have selected and give students background regarding this business. Explain your reasons for writing this letter and your desire to receive a letter in response.

2. Once the purpose of the letter has been determined, discuss the format of how to write a letter. Explain to students that each letter has different parts. The parts of a letter are the heading, greeting, body, and closing. On the overhead projector, place the transparency of the model letter and review it with the students. Point out each part of the letter and read the letter aloud. Explain to students that you will use these same parts of a letter in your class letter.

3. Tape a piece of chart paper to the whiteboard or chalkboard. Brainstorm as a class the things that should be included in the letter. Record these onto the chart paper with the marking pen.

4. Tape another piece of chart paper to the whiteboard or chalkboard. Using the marking pen, begin writing the letter. Remember to begin with the heading and proceed in that manner. Encourage students to participate in the writing of the letter. Use the ideas and notes recorded. When finished, read the letter, and edit it for punctuation, capitalization, and spelling. Fold up the chart paper and place it in the envelope. Ask students what is needed for this letter to be mailed. Place the postage and the address on the envelope, modeling both for the students. Look for a response in the mail!

5. Explain to students that they are now ready to write a letter of their own. Go through this same procedure to walk students through their own letter. Use the "Letter Format" on page 64 as a guide.

Model Letter

Read the letter below as a class. Discuss the parts of a letter. The parts of this letter include a heading, a greeting, the body, signature, and a closing.

Heading

September 4, 2008

Greeting

Dear Mr. Garner,

Body

We are writing this letter to ask permission to come and visit your grocery store. We would like to come and learn about how a grocery store works. Do you think that you would be available to visit with us?

We would like to see the departments in the grocery store. The departments we would like to see are the meat department, produce department, floral department, and the dairy department.

The day that we would like to come is Friday, September 25. Please write back and let us know if this is a good day for us to visit. Thank you for reading our letter. We hope to hear from you soon!

Sincerely, *Closing*

Mrs. Baker *Signature*

Mrs. Baker

Letter Format

Use this letter format to direct students when writing a letter. This letter format will assist students in writing a letter of their own.

Dear —————————————————,

—————————————————————————————

—————————————————————————————

—————————————————————————————

—————————————————————————————

—————————————————————————————

—————————————————————————————

—————————————————————————————

—————————————————————————————

————————————————,

————————————————

Letter Sample

A first grade student at the beginning of the school year wrote this sample letter. The text is readable by adults who are familiar with phonetic spelling. It is made up of words which are, for the most part, represented by appropriate initial and final consonants. There are some letter reversals. The text echoes oral language. The text consists of one long sentence. The heading was omitted, but the letter contains a greeting, body, and closing.

Dier St. Nick I yot
A soccer ball ANd
I yot yuo To gif A
FAmLey that dusit haf
ine food Food ANd I
WANT you To gif
cids that dad haf
Tus Tus.

From TristAN

(Dear St. Nick,

I want a soccer ball and I want you to give a family that doesn't have any food, food and I want you to give kids that don't have toys, toys.

From Tristan)

Expository Writing

Use this lesson to introduce expository writing. The objective of this lesson is to complete an expository writing piece as a class.

Materials

- chart paper
- marking pen
- several books on selected topic
- copy of "Expository Idea Graph for Beginning Writers" (page 68)
- "Sentence Frames" (page 67)

Preparation

Select a topic to write about that is important to the children. Collect several books on the topic.

Directions

1. Discuss expository writing with students. Expository writing gives information, describes or explains something, or defines the meaning of something. Expository pieces can be developed in a variety of ways. Beginning expository pieces use facts and data, while more advanced expository writing is developed by comparison-contrast, cause and effect, and through examples. It's important to understand that expository writing is usually unemotional and is written in third person. This is very new to early and emergent writers who are used to writing about themselves and in the first person.

2. Expository writing should:

    - state the purpose and topic
    - explain
    - include facts, give reasons, and/or give examples

3. Begin by discussing the selected topic with the students. Show the books over a period of days. Read and discuss the topic in detail. Illicit the background knowledge of your students using a K-W-L (**K**now-**W**ant to Know-**L**earned) chart. As you read the books, model taking notes by recording responses on the chart paper. Use the "Expository Idea Graph for Beginning Writers" on page 68 to help record ideas.

4. Model aloud how to use the information gathered to write an expository piece. Use the notes and background knowledge to write the report. Select a title for the report. When it is complete, read and reread the piece. Call on input from the students. Is there information that needs to be added or deleted? Is there enough information?

5. When the drafting stage has been completed, type up the expository piece on the computer. Print it out and give each student one of the pages. Each student or group of students should be given a page to illustrate. Don't forget a cover page. When finished, read the report again as a class. Explain to students that they are now ready to write a report of their own. Go through this same procedure to walk students through their own expository piece. Use the sentence frames on page 67 as a guide.

Sentence Frames

Use the following topics and frame sentences to get ideas for expository writing:

Topic: Animals
- This animal eats _____
- This animal lives _____
- This animal's body is covered with _____
- This animal moves by _____
- This animal's babies are called _____
- Interesting facts about this animal are _____

Topic: Foods
- Nutritious foods are _____
- Unhealthy foods are _____
- Examples of vegetables are _____
- Examples of fruits are _____
- Examples of grains are _____
- Examples of dairy products are _____
- Examples of meats are _____
- Favorite foods to eat are _____
- Our bodies need food because _____

Topic: Dinosaurs
- This dinosaur had _____
- This dinosaur lived during the _____
- This dinosaur walked on _____ feet.
- This dinosaur's nickname was _____
- This dinosaur was as big as _____
- This dinosaur ate _____
- Interesting facts about this dinosaur are _____

Topic: Places to Travel
- This place is _____ miles from home.
- You can do _____ at this place.
- You will need to bring _____ to travel here.

Topic: How to Do Something
- First Step: _____
- Second Step: _____
- Third Step: _____
- Fourth Step: _____
- Finally: _____

Expository Idea Graph
for Beginning Writers

*(**Teacher Note:** Each circle on this graph represents a fact and a sentence for the expository text. You may need to adjust the number of circles needed for students. This page can be used as a brainstorming page or a place to record facts.)*

Name: _____

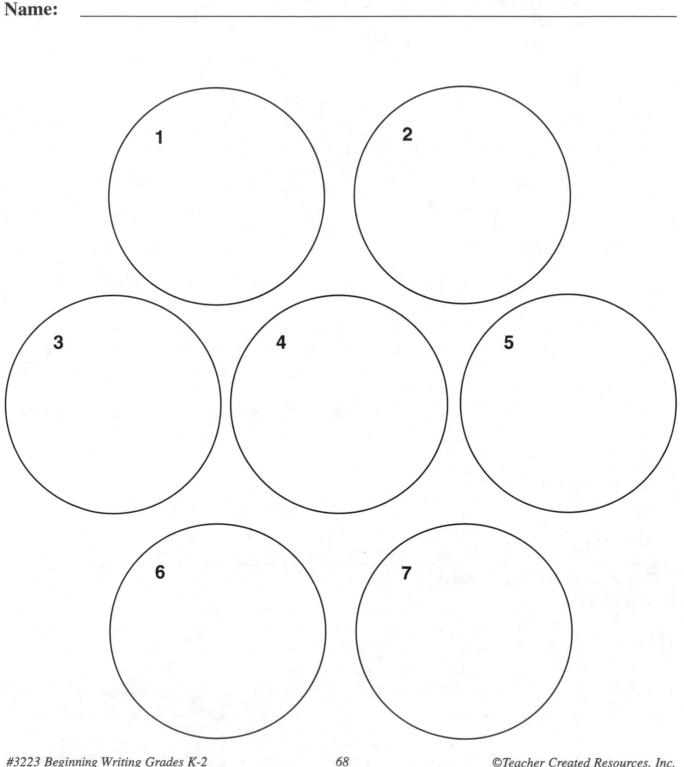

Expository Sample

A kindergarten student at the midpoint of the school year wrote this sample of expository writing. The student uses complete sentences with proper capitalization and punctuation. The student spells many high-frequency words correctly. The student uses a title to begin this expository text. The student identifies four facts about polar bears.

PolarBears

PolarBearscan run.
PolarBearscanswim
PolarBears havecubs.
PolarBearscaneatgras

(Polar Bears

Polar bears can run. Polar bears can swim. Polar bears have cubs.
Polar bears can eat grass.)

Language Use and Conventions

As a teacher, there are times that you wish you could teach a lesson that focuses on a specific skill your students need. This section of the unit is meant to help you do just that. Select the lessons in this section that will help improve the writing skills of your students. There are lessons on punctuation, how to write a sentence, spelling, descriptive language, and other language use and conventions.

The following terms and words are used in this unit. Use the guide below to assist students in learning and understanding the meaning of these words.

Declarative Sentences

Declarative sentences make a statement. These are also called "telling sentences."
Examples: The girl is holding a doll.
        I can sing.

Interrogative Sentences

Interrogative sentences ask a question. These are also called "asking sentences" or questions.
Examples: Are you in Kindergarten?
        Where is your house?

Nouns

A *noun* is a person, place, or thing. A noun is who or what a sentence is about.
Examples: (*person*) Taylor likes ice cream.
        (*place*) Arizona is a desert state.
        (*thing*) Where is my pencil?

Verbs

A *verb* is the action part of the sentence.
Examples: The boy jumps.
        The dog barked.

Adjectives

An *adjective* is a describing word. An adjective describes a noun.
Examples: The cat is soft.
        The leaf is green.
        The elephant is big.

Period

A *period* is used at the end of a declarative or a "telling" sentence.
Example: I am happy.

Question Mark

A *question mark* is used at the end of an interrogative sentence or a question.
Examples: Where are we?
        What is that noise?

What Is a Sentence?

At this stage, most students can speak complete sentences, but not always write them. With a little instruction, your most novice writer can begin to write sentences.

Materials

- chalkboard or whiteboard
- chalk or whiteboard markers

Preparation

Write a sentence that students can read on the chalkboard or whiteboard prior to the start of the lesson.

Directions

Explain to the students that a sentence is a group of words that tell about something. A sentence tells about a person, place, or thing doing something. Read aloud the sentence you have written on the board. Invite the students to read the sentence with you. As students read, point to each word.

Sample: The   boy   ran.

Now you are ready to analyze the sentence. Ask the students who the sentence is about. The sentence is about the boy. Circle the word <u>boy</u>, and write <u>who</u> or <u>what</u>? Noun.

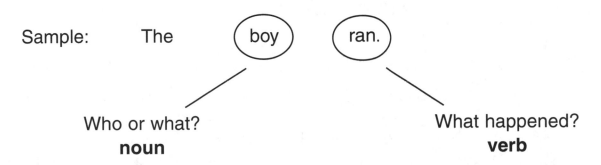

Write another sentence on the board. Ask students to identify who or what the sentence is about and what happened. Label the sentence in the same manner. Write three more sentences following the same procedure to give students practice. Be sure that the sentences you select are very simple and short. Long sentences can be confusing at this stage. Then write fragments on the board. For example, write the word, "ran." Explain that this is not a sentence. It does not tell us who ran. Now write the words, "The boy." Explain that this is not a sentence either because it doesn't tell us what happened to the boy.

Point out the period at the end of the sentence. Explain to the students that putting a period at the end of the sentence shows the reader that it is a sentence. Call on students to come to the board to find the periods in all of the sentences on the board.

From now on, you can ask students to locate sentences and periods in their reading and writing activities. Be active in your search of locating sentences and periods. Always talk aloud about putting a period at the end of your sentences and remind students to include sentences and periods in their writing.

Tell Me Something

Once you have given basic instruction on what a sentence is and how to write a sentence (see page 71), students are ready to practice writing their own sentences.

Materials

- paper
- ball
- pencils, crayons, or colored pencils

Directions

Review with students what a sentence is, how to write one, and how to punctuate a declarative sentence. Write sample sentences like these on the board:

The girl is jumping.

The box is opened.

The clown is laughing.

I am singing.

For each sentence, have students identify the noun (subject) and the verb. These sentences tell something. They are called "telling" sentences. Another name for these sentences is *declarative*.

Instruct students to form a circle. Go around the circle taking turns to tell something. The student must state a declarative sentence. After each student responds, ask the class to identify the noun and the verb in each sentence. Then ask students what goes at the end of a sentence? A period!

Once you have gone around the circle, add a ball to the mix. Begin rolling the ball to a student. This student shares a sentence and then rolls the ball to another student in the circle. This student continues in the same manner. Students must be ready at any time to share a sentence with the class. The ball continues rolling around the circle. Record some of the sentences on the board for future analysis.

✏ Independent Practice

After the game, analyze the sentences you wrote on the board as a class. Help students identify the nouns, verbs, and the periods at the end. Distribute paper and pencils to the students. Have students write down five sentences. Circulate the room to assist students as needed. Not all students may be able to complete the activity independently. You may need to pair students up, as necessary, or provide volunteers to assist students.

After writing each sentence, have students circle the noun, the verb, and the period at the end. When students have finished writing down five sentences, they should illustrate these sentences using crayons or colored pencils. If time allows, students can share their sentences with a partner, small group, or with the whole class.

Put It All Together!

A sentence is a complete thought with a noun, a verb, and a punctuation mark at the end. Match the groups of words to make sentences. Write the sentences on the lines below.

1.	The snake	moos.
2.	The rabbit	buzzes.
3.	The lion	chirps.
4.	The dog	jumps.
5.	The bee	barks.
6.	The bird	slithers.
7.	The cow	roars.

1. _____

2. _____

3. _____

4. _____

5. _____

6. _____

7. _____

What Is a Question?

Another type of sentence that students will use in their writing is interrogative sentences. This lesson will teach students to recognize interrogative sentences and identify question marks.

Materials

- paper and pencil (for each student)
- chalkboard or whiteboard
- chalk or whiteboard markers
- large bowl
- index cards with the following words: *Who, What, Where, Does, When, Why, How, May, Do, Are, Is, Can, Would, Should,* and *Could.*

Directions

1. Explain to students that you would like to teach them about a new type of sentence. An interrogative sentence asks a question. Read the examples below:

   What time is it?

   Where is my cat?

   Why am I here?

2. Write these three sentences on the board. Read each sentence aloud. Ask students to read each sentence with you. Point to each word as you read the sentence.

3. When finished, ask students to identify something new in these sentences. Ask students, "What comes at the end of these sentences?" It looks different than a period.

4. Explain to the students that this is a question mark. A question mark comes at the end of an asking sentence. Demonstrate on the board how to make a question mark. Distribute paper and pencils to students and instruct students to practice making question marks.

5. Instruct students that there are words that go at the beginning of interrogative or asking sentences. Hold up each of the index cards with the question words written on them. Place all of the index cards in a bowl. Have each student draw a card from the bowl. The student must ask a question using the word on the card. Proceed around the circle until everyone has had a turn.

6. As an extension of this activity, you can divide your class into small groups. Write a sentence on index cards placing one word on each card. Give each group a pile of index cards that make up a sentence. Students should work together to read the cards, and place them in order so that the words form a sentence. Remember to put a question mark on one of the cards. Students must remember to put the question mark at the end of the sentence before they are done.

Descriptive Language

Teaching students about descriptive language can motivate students to use more of it in their writing. Use this lesson to teach and practice using adjectives and descriptive language.

Materials

- chart paper
- colored marker
- paper lunch bags (1 per student)
- stapler

Preparation

Prepare a sample bag prior to the lesson. Write your name on the bag. Select an object to put inside the bag. Write five adjectives on the bag that describe the item. Place the item in the bag and staple it closed. Plan to spend at least two days on this lesson.

Directions

1. On the first day, begin by reading a story aloud to the class that uses a lot of descriptive language. (See the bibliography on page 80 for suggestions.) When finished reading, ask the students to tell you descriptive words from the story. Make a list of these descriptive words on the board.

2. Now show the students your sample bag. Read the descriptive words on the bag. Explain to the students that these descriptive words are called adjectives. Ask students, "Will the words written on this bag help me figure out what is inside the bag?" The answer is "yes" because the words are describing what is in the bag.

3. Call on students to guess what is inside the bag. After a few minutes, open the bag and show the students the object. Point out how each of the adjectives written on the bag describes the item.

4. Instruct students to locate an item in the classroom that is small enough to fit inside of the bag. Once the object has been selected, have each student return to his or her desk and write five adjectives or descriptive words on the bag. (You may need to have volunteers on hand to help.) Once the five words have been written, each student then places the item in the bag and with help, staples the bag closed.

5. On the second day, have the students share their bags. As they tell their adjectives, instruct the other students to listen. The child who is sharing can call on children to make guesses about the object inside. Have the student open the bag to reveal the contents.

6. Add the students' adjectives to the class chart you began on the previous day. Continue to add adjectives to the chart, as desired. Encourage the children to use these and other adjectives in their writing.

Capitalization

Capital letters are used at the beginning of each sentence. (If your students are ready, discuss capitalization used with proper nouns.) Review the examples below.

My horse is brown and gray.

We got to go to the store.

She is my sister.

My mother likes soup.

These sentences are missing capital letters. Write the sentences correctly.

1. grandma is coming to our house. _____

_____

2. mrs. jones is my teacher. _____

_____

3. where are we? _____

_____

4. open the door, please _____

_____

5. can you find my shoe? _____

_____

6. today is friday. _____

_____

7. are you nice. _____

_____

8. here is your present. _____

_____

Write two sentences of your own. Don't forget the capital letter!

1. _____

2. _____

Do It in Five!

Select one of the activities below to do as a class. These activities will help students practice using capitals, periods, and question marks. Each activity should take no more than five minutes. You may need to adjust the number of sentences required for students in your class.

Write the sentences below. Use the correct punctuation mark for each sentence.

1. I like my new house _____

   _____

2. Where are we going _____

   _____

3. She is my friend _____

   _____

Write the sentences below correctly. Put the capital at the beginning of each sentence.

1. john is coming to my house. _____

   _____

2. are you happy? _____

   _____

3. we watched a movie. _____

   _____

Group Work

1. Divide your class into small groups. Give each student a pencil or highlighter marker. Distribute newspapers or old magazines to each group of students. Students in each group should highlight or underline any punctuation or capitalization they see.

2. Divide your class into two teams. On the chalkboard, write a sentence that is missing the punctuation mark or a capital letter. Each student sends a team member to the board to write the sentence correctly.

Home-School Activities

There are so many things that parents can do to reinforce writing lessons and skills taught in school. Encourage this parental support by suggesting home-school activities from the next two pages for your students and parents. These activities are considered optional.

✐ Let's Talk About It

Invite your child to talk to you about writing projects they have been working on at school. Be sure to make eye contact and listen to what your child is saying. When finished, ask your child questions. Be sure to ask your child frequently about what they have written. This not only allows your child to think about his or her writing, but it validates the work your child is doing at school.

✐ Researching the News

Look for ideas to research when reading the newspaper, magazines, or watching television. Keep a folder of notes, clipping, and other information on topics in which your family has an interest. Have your child be in charge of the folder. Discuss the news items or other topics over the dinner table or on car trips. Keep an attitude of learning alive in your home—it's contagious!

✐ Story Swap

Give each member of your family a piece of paper. Have each person begin writing a story. After a few minutes, switch papers with each other. Now add to each other's stories. Continue switching papers until each family member has had a turn to add to each story and the story has an ending. Share the stories aloud. Be prepared for some laughs and giggles as the stories take unexpected turns.

✐ Topic Charades

Write research topics or topics of interest on slips of paper. Family members draw a slip of paper and act out what is written on the paper, using the information they already know about the topic. What do other family members know about the subject? Spend time discussing the topic before moving on to the next charade.

✐ Question Query

Ask questions as a family and research the answers in encyclopedias, on the Internet, or from other resources. Using email, ask questions of friends and family members who might be able to answer questions. Spend time discussing the questions and the different ways that answers can be found.

✐ Show and Tell

When your child brings home a rough draft or piece of writing, set aside some quiet time to let your child share this piece of writing with you. Read it together, and ask questions. Provide positive feedback on your child's writing abilities and progress. Take time to share writing that you have recently done, with your child. This might be a business report, a letter, a note, or a request. Explain to your child how you used writing and explain the purpose of the writing.

Home-School Activities *(cont.)*

✏ Expert for the Day

Set aside a place at the dinner table for an expert to visit your family. Tell the family that you have invited an expert on a specific topic to come and share information with the family. Spend the dinner with this "expert" asking questions and sharing information. Set up another day and invite an expert from your own family. Discuss a topic of interest with your expert. Be sure to have a day when every family member is the expert. Everyone is an expert at something!

✏ Parent-Child Journals

Create a journal by stapling pages together or using a notebook. The journal is simple. Begin by writing a note to your child. Have your child read the letter and respond by writing a letter to you. Continue in this manner on a daily or a weekly basis. You will learn many things about your child and you will encourage writing in the process! Your parent-child relationship will be strengthened.

✏ Use Your Senses

Talk with your child about the senses of sight, sound, smell, taste, and touch. Ask your child to tell you what they learn from using their senses. How do senses help us learn about the world in which we live? Is there one sense that we rely on more than the others? How do we use our senses to eat, for safety, for learning, adventure, mobility, etc.?

✏ Dictionary Fun

Pull out the dictionary at your house and spend an evening perusing it with your child. Look at the different words that can be found in the dictionary. Allow your child time to ask questions and make observations about the different words. Encourage your child to think of a word that he or she would like to look up in the dictionary. Assist him or her in finding the word and reading the definition. Show your child where the pronunciation of each word can be found and the part of speech. Discuss the meaning of this word and use the word in a sentence.

✏ ABC at Home

Write each letter of the alphabet on a piece of paper. Have your child go throughout the house and find items that begin with that letter. See if your child can find an item for each letter of the alphabet.

✏ Newsy News

Give your child a highlighter marker and an old newspaper or magazine. Using the marker, have your child highlight when a capital letter, or a period was used. Review with your child the times when a capital letter and a period are needed.

Bibliography

Books

Caulkins, Lucy. *The Art of Teaching Writing*. Heinemann, 1982.

Duke, Kate. *Aunt Isabel Tells a Good One*. Dutton Children's Books, 1992.

Graves, Donald and Virginia Stuart. *Write From the Start*. Dutton, 1985.

Heller, Ruth. *Many Luscious Lollipops: A Book About Adjectives*. Putnam Publishing Group, 1991.

McClanahan, Elaine and Carolyn Wicks. *Future Force: Kids That Want To, Can and Do*. Griffin Publishing, 1994.

Silberman, Arlene. *Growing up Writing: Teaching Children to Write, Think, and Learn*. Time Books, 1989.

Unwin, Charlotte. *Let's Pretend*. Dial Books for Young Readers, 1989.

Vogler, Christopher. The Writer's Journey: *Mythic Structure of Storytellers and Screenwriters*. Michael Wiese Productions, 1992.

Useful Web Sites

- *http://www.theteacherscorner.net/*
  This Web page features a variety of lesson plans for teaching stories to younger children.

- *http://www.thewritesource.com/topics.htm*
  Grade level appropriate writing topics and ideas for students

- *http://www.fwsd.wednet.edu/cur/targets/K/index.html*
  This Web page features examples of Kindergarten writing.

- *http://www.3sk.sympatico.ca/fiss/newspage1.html*
  This Web site teaches how to use the writing process in your classroom.

- *http://mgfx.com/kidlit/*
  This Web page is designed for kids. It includes student book reviews and short stories written by kids.

- *http://www.enchantedlearning.com/Dictionary.html*
  Online dictionary for youngsters

- *http://www.canteach.ca/elementary/beginning.html*
  This Web site has a story-writing game and other lesson plans that involve computer use.